SPORTING CHAMPIONSHIPS
SUPER BOWL

Aneel Brar

WEIGL PUBLISHERS INC.

Published by Weigl Publishers Inc.
350 5th Avenue, Suite 3304, PMB 6G
New York, NY 10118-0069

Website: www.weigl.com

Library of Congress Cataloging-in-Publication Data

Brar, Aneel.
  Super Bowl / Aneel Brar.
    p. cm. -- (Sporting championships)
  Includes index.
  ISBN 978-1-59036-689-9 (hard cover : alk. paper) -- ISBN 978-1-59036-690-5 (soft cover : alk. paper)
  1. Super Bowl--Juvenile literature. 2. Super Bowl--History--Juvenile literature. 3. Football--History--Juvenile literature. I. Title.
  GV956.2.S8B73 2008
  796.332'648--dc22

                                    2007012100

Printed in the United States of America
1 2 3 4 5 6 7 8 9 0 11 10 09 08 07

Project Coordinator
James Duplacey

Design
Terry Paulhus

CONTENTS

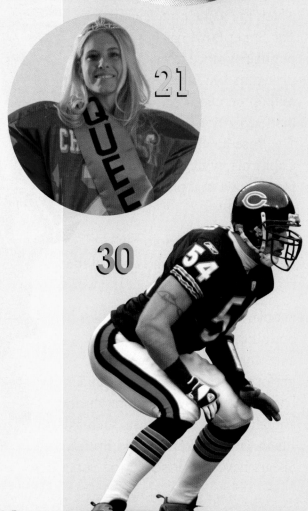

What is the Super Bowl?

The Super Bowl is the championship game of the National Football League (NFL). It is played between the best team from the American Football Conference (AFC) and the best team from the National Football Conference (NFC). The game is always played on a Sunday. This day is called Super Bowl Sunday.

On Super Bowl Sunday, thousands of people pack the stadium where the game is played. More than 100 million people watch the game on television. The Super Bowl has grown in popularity since it was first played in 1967. More than 65 million people watched the first Super Bowl on television. The Rose Bowl, in Pasedena, California, where the first Super Bowl was played, was not full.

Today, the game is sold out months in advance. It is one of the biggest sporting events in the world.

People watch the Super Bowl for both the football and the entertainment. There are live performances by music stars and bands. They perform before, during, and after the game. Artists such as Justin Timberlake, U2, and Britney Spears have performed at the Super Bowl.

In the 41-year history of the Super Bowl, no team has been able to win the game in its home stadium.

Special television commercials are made just for the game. Millions of viewers watch the game just to see these commercials. Football fans from more than 100 countries watch the game on television every year.

CHANGES THROUGHOUT THE YEARS	
Past	**Present**
A 30-second television commerical cost $42,000.	A 30-second television commerical costs more than $2.6 million.
Six officials were used in the Super Bowl.	Seven officials are used in the Super Bowl.
The top-priced ticket cost $12.	The top-priced ticket costs more than $750.
The referees' jerseys had numbers on the sleeves.	The referees' jerseys have numbers on the back.

The Vince Lombardi Trophy

The Super Bowl champions are awarded the Vince Lombardi Trophy. Vince Lombardi coached the Green Bay Packers to victory in the first two Super Bowls. The trophy stands 22 inches (55 centimeters) tall and weighs 7 pounds (3 kilograms). It consists of a life-sized football made of sterling silver mounted on a tall, triangle-shaped base. The words "Vince Lombardi Trophy" and the NFL logo are engraved on the trophy. The winning team gets to keep the trophy. A new one is made each year.

Super Bowl History

The Super Bowl was not always called the Super Bowl. The first three Super Bowl games were known as the AFL-NFL World Championship Games.

For many years, the National Football League was the only professional league in the United States. In 1960, another professional football league was formed. The American Football League (AFL) had eight teams. The AFL introduced new rules, such as the two-point convert. After a team scored a touchdown, it could try to run or pass the ball into the **end zone** for an extra two points. Top college stars, such as Joe Namath and Lance Alworth, joined the new league instead of the NFL.

The Kansas City Chiefs were originally based in Dallas, Texas. The team moved to Kansas City in 1963 and won the AFL championship in 1966.

The AFL had a major television contract. This meant their games were seen by millions of fans. The NFL and AFL competed with each other for players and fans for much of the 1960s. In 1966, it was announced that the AFL and NFL would combine into a single league. The move would take place in 1970. It was decided that there would be a championship game between the top team in each league. The first game took place on January 15, 1967. The Green Bay Packers defeated the Kansas City Chiefs 35–10 at the Los Angeles Memorial Coliseum. More than 60,000 fans attended the game.

Lamar Hunt, the president of the AFL, was the person who thought of the name Super Bowl. Hunt saw his children playing with a toy called a super ball. It was a lively rubber ball that bounced wildly. Since championship games in college football are often called bowl games, Hunt decided to call the AFL-NFL championship game the Super Bowl. It soon became the official name for the game. In 1971, the first three AFL-NFL World Championship Games were re-named Super Bowl I, II, and III.

The Denver Broncos were one of the original AFL franchises that began play in 1960. Quarterback John Elway helped the team to the Super Bowl title in 1998 and 1999.

Football Mascots

Twenty-seven of the 32 teams in the NFL have mascots. Many have original names and costumes. The Cincinnati Bengals' mascot is Who Dey. He was named after the team cheer, "Who dey! Who dey! Who dey think gonna beat dem Bengals?" The Baltimore Ravens have three mascots named Edgar, Allen, and Poe. They are named after well-known Baltimore poet Edgar Allen Poe. Freddy Falcon has been the official mascot of the Atlanta Falcons for 35 years. He was the first sports mascot in the city of Atlanta.

Rules of the Game

The rules of football have changed since the game was first played. Many of the changes were made to increase scoring and make the game more fun to watch and play. Others have helped make the game safer for the players.

1 The Game
A football game has four quarters. Each quarter is 15 minutes long. The game has two 30-minute halves. If the score is tied, a 15-minute overtime period is played. The team that scores first wins.

2 Moving the Ball
The offense runs or throws the ball to move it down the field. The offense has four chances, or downs, to move the ball at least ten yards. If they gain ten yards, they get four more downs. They keep the ball until they score, fail to gain 10 yards, or lose possession of the ball because of a **fumble** or **interception**.

3 The Clock
While a team has the ball, they have 40 seconds to make a play. The clock stops when a forward pass is not caught or the player with the ball steps out of bounds. The clock will stop if a penalty is called. Teams can stop the clock three times in each half. These are called timeouts. The clock also stops when there are two minutes left in each half. This is known as the two-minute warning.

The play clock tells players how long they have to put the ball in play.

4 Line of Scrimmage

At the **snap** of the ball, there must be at least seven offensive players on the **line of scrimmage**. Players not on the line of scrimmage must be at least one yard behind it. If a player moves before the snap of the ball, an **offside** penalty is called.

5 Scoring

If a team carries the ball into the end zone, a touchdown worth six points is scored. After scoring a touchdown, a team can try to score extra points. This is called a convert. There are two ways to score extra points. Teams can kick the ball through the uprights or goal posts. This is worth a single point. Teams can also try to carry or pass the ball into the end zone after a touchdown has been scored. This is worth an extra two points.

Making the Call

There are seven officials on the field during the Super Bowl. Every official can call a penalty, but the head referee makes the final decision on all rulings. The umpire watches for fouls or penalties. The head linesman and line judge ensure players do not move before the snap of the ball. Field judges and side judges decide if the ball has been caught. The back judge ensures that each side has only 11 players on the field.

The Football Field

The game of football is played on a rectangular field that is 100 yards (91.4 meters) long and 53.5 yards (49 m) wide. At each end of the playing field are two 10-yard (9.1-m) areas called end zones. There are lines that run parallel to the goal line and across the field. These lines help measure how far the football has moved on the field. They establish the line of scrimmage.

Two sets of short lines run down the left and right side of the field. These are called hash marks. They are used as guides to show where the ball should be placed on the field. Each play in football starts between or on the hash marks.

Sideline yard markers tell players and fans where the ball is on the playing field.

The line that separates the main field from the end zone is called the goal line. The object of the game is to put the ball inside the end zone. A touchdown is scored when the ball is carried across this line. On the back line of each end zone are the goal posts. They are often called uprights. Points are scored when the football is kicked through the goal posts.

Most outdoor football fields are made of natural grass. Football can be played inside covered stadiums. Real grass cannot grow in these stadiums. These fields have artificial grass, called turf. It is made of a mixture of **synthetic** materials, such as sand and rubber. It looks and feels like real grass.

Players on the Team

A football team has an offensive team and a defensive team. Each team has 11 players. The offensive linemen protect the quarterback. The quarterback calls the plays and passes or hands the ball to a teammate. The running backs and fullbacks run, block, and catch the ball. The tight end and wide receivers catch passes. The defensive linemen attack the opposing team's quarterback. Linebackers try to stop the other team from rushing or running with the football. Cornerbacks and safeties try to stop the opposition from catching passes and scoring touchdowns.

FOOTBALL FIELD

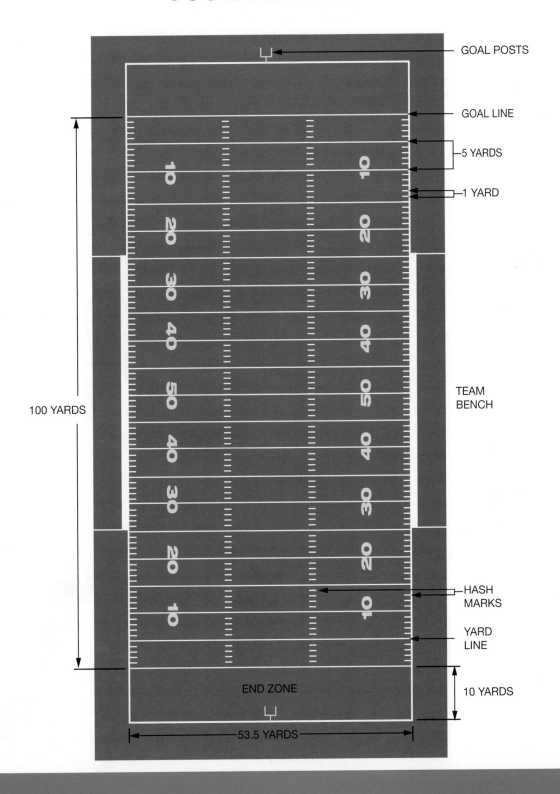

GOAL POSTS

GOAL LINE

5 YARDS

1 YARD

100 YARDS

TEAM BENCH

HASH MARKS

YARD LINE

END ZONE

10 YARDS

53.5 YARDS

Football Equipment

Football equipment is designed to protect the player from injury. The football helmet is made of hard plastic. It is lined with inflatable air cushions. The helmet cushions the impact of a blow to the head from another player or from the ground. The helmet has a face guard with two or three metal bars to protect the face.

Shoulder pads are made of hard plastic and lined with foam. Different shoulder pads are made for each position. Linebackers have big pads because they hit and get hit more than other players. Receivers often wear lightweight pads so they can run and catch the ball easier.

Football **cleats** give players better traction. This helps them change direction quickly and avoid hits without slipping. Players wear tight football pants with thigh, hip, and knee pads. These pads help protect the players when they get hit or tackled by the opposing team.

Helmet

Face guard

Gloves

Thigh pads

Linebacker

Shoes with cleats

GET CONNECTED

Learn more about football equipment at **www.howstuffworks. com.** Put "football equipment" in search engine.

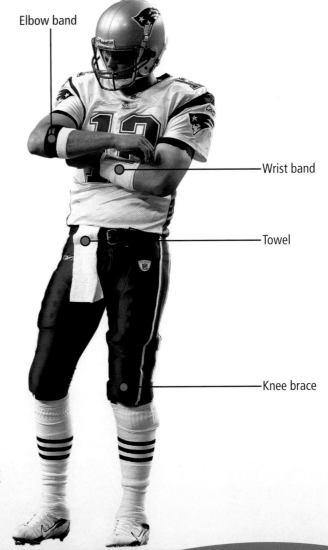

Elbow band

Wrist band

Towel

Knee brace

Quarterback

Most players wear gloves to help them grip the ball when it is wet and muddy. When teams play on artifical turf, many players wear tape on their forearms and elbows. This protects the players' arms from getting scraped or burned when the player falls on the turf.

Quarterbacks often hang a towel from the waistband of their football pants to dry their hands. Most quarterbacks wear a wristband that has the **plays** they are going to call written on it. Some quarterbacks wear bands made of elastic or rubber on their arms to support their elbows. Many quarterbacks wear extra pads to protect their ribs.

Team Uniforms

Home teams in the NFL often wear dark jerseys. The visiting team often wears a white jersey. Many NFL teams have a third jersey that can only be worn twice a year. To mark a special moment in the history of the franchise, NFL teams can wear a throwback, or historical jersey.

Jersey numbers are important in football. They help officials keep track of where players are on the field. Quarterbacks can only wear numbers 1–19, running backs 20–49, centers and linebackers 50–59, defensive linemen and offensive linemen 60–79, and wide receivers and tight ends 80–89.

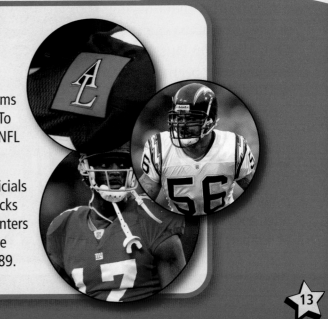

Qualifying to Play

Teams in the NFL play 16 regular-season games over 17 weeks. The two conferences in the NFL, the AFC and the NFC, each have four divisions. There are four teams in each division. Teams compete to win their respective divisions and conferences by getting the most regular-season wins. The better a team does in the regular season, the more advantages it will have in the playoffs.

The NFL playoffs begin when the regular season is finished. The season usually finishes at the end of December. Only 12 teams make the playoffs. The four division champions from the AFC and NFC always qualify.

The two teams that have the best regular-season win-loss records get a first-round **bye**. This means

Only four wild card teams—Oakland, Denver, Pittsburgh, and Baltimore—have been able to win the Super Bowl.

that they will get a week of rest before they play their first playoff game. They also get the advantage of playing at home when they play. This is called the home field advantage. It is difficult to win the Super Bowl without having at least one home game. Only the 2006 Pittsburgh Steelers have been able to do this.

The road to the Super Bowl is a month-long journey that often ends in the first week of February.

An additional two teams from each conference make the playoffs. They are known as wild card teams. These are teams with the fifth and sixth best regular-season records.

The wild card teams play the teams with the third and fourth best records in the regular season. This first round of the playoffs is called the wild card round.

The winners of these wild card games play the remaining division champions in the divisional round. Then, the winners of the divisional round games play against each other. The winners of this round are named AFC and NFC conference champions.

The two conference champions play each other in the Super Bowl. There is often a two-week break between the conference finals and the Super Bowl. The championship game is usually played in the first week of February.

The Pittsburgh Steelers won their fifth Super Bowl title when they defeated the Seattle Seahawks 21–10 in Super Bowl XL.

Super Bowl Rings

Every year, the players on the winning team at the Super Bowl get a ring to mark their victory. These rings are often covered in diamonds. Each ring has the team logo and the individual player's name and number engraved on it.

The New England Patriots won Super Bowl XXXIX. They had the Vince Lombardi Trophy engraved on their rings. The San Francisco 49ers had a pair of Vince Lombardi Trophies engraved on their rings after they won Super Bowl XIX. This was done to mark their two Super Bowl victories.

Where They Play

Movies, Music, and Hollywood was the theme of the pre-game show before Super Bowl XXVII. Garth Brooks sang the national anthem, and Michael Jackson was the featured performer during the halftime show.

The site of each Super Bowl is decided years ahead of time. Cities around the United States compete for the honor. The Super Bowl can bring in more than $300 to $400 million to the host city.

Not every city can host the Super Bowl. The host city must have a stadium that can seat more than 65,000 people. The average temperature in that city has to be at least 50 degrees Fahrenheit (10 degrees Celsius) in February. There are charity events, football clinics, and press conferences. The city needs quality hotels for the teams and spectators as well as places to hold all of the events. These hotels must be within a one-hour drive of the stadium. The city must have three golf courses that can be used for the NFL's annual charity golf tournament. The Dallas Cowboys have played in a record eight Super Bowl games but have never hosted the championship game. Their stadium does not seat enough people.

The Rose Bowl in Pasadena, California, has hosted the Super Bowl five times.

The NFL has made exceptions to these rules. Cold-weather cities, such as Detroit and Minneapolis, have hosted Super Bowls because they had covered stadiums. It does not matter what the weather is like outside the stadium.

Miami, Florida, and New Orleans, Louisiana have each hosted the Super Bowl nine times. The city of Glendale, Arizona, hosted its first Super Bowl in 2008. The game will return to Tampa, Florida, for the third time in 2009. Miami, Florida, has been chosen to host the Super Bowl for a record tenth time in 2010.

Most Super Bowl games have been played in outdoor stadiums with natural grass fields, such as Dolphin Stadium in Miami, Florida.

The NFL has played regular-season games in Mexico City, Mexico, and London, England. However, there are no plans to hold a Super Bowl game outside the United States.

SUPER BOWL WINNERS 1997–2007				
YEAR	CITY	WINNING TEAM	SCORE	LOSING TEAM
1997	New Orleans	Green Bay Packers	35–21	New England Patriots
1998	San Diego	Denver Broncos	31–24	Green Bay Packers
1999	Miami	Denver Broncos	31–19	Atlanta Falcons
2000	Atlanta	St. Louis Rams	23–16	Tennessee Titans
2001	Tampa	Baltimore Ravens	34–7	New York Giants
2002	New Orleans	New England Patriots	20–17	St. Louis Rams
2003	San Diego	Tampa Bay Buccaneers	48–21	Oakland Raiders
2004	Houston	New England Patriots	32–29	Carolina Panthers
2005	Jacksonville	New England Patriots	24–21	Philadelphia Eagles
2006	Detroit	Pittsburgh Steelers	21–10	Seattle Seahawks
2007	Miami	Indianapolis Colts	29–17	Chicago Bears

Mapping the Super Bowl

The National Football League has 32 teams in the United States. Match the team in the chart with the circled number on this map to find out where each of these NFL teams are located.

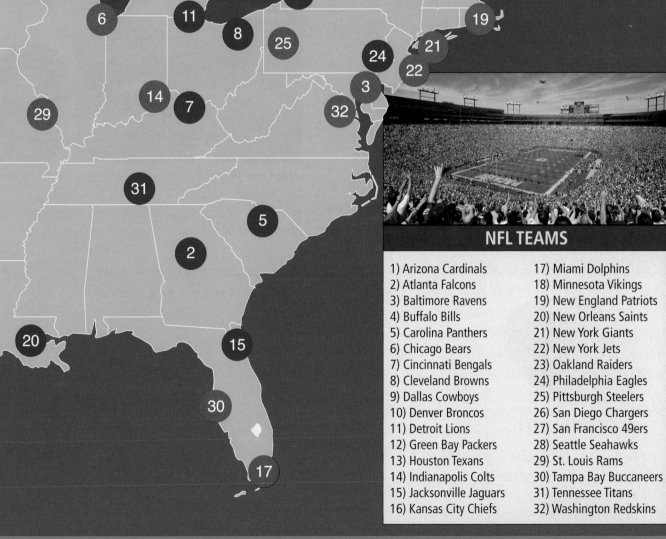

LEGEND

● NFL teams that have won the Super Bowl

● NFL teams that have not won the Super Bowl

N
W   E
S

Scale   621 Miles

0   1,000 Kilometers

NFL TEAMS

1) Arizona Cardinals
2) Atlanta Falcons
3) Baltimore Ravens
4) Buffalo Bills
5) Carolina Panthers
6) Chicago Bears
7) Cincinnati Bengals
8) Cleveland Browns
9) Dallas Cowboys
10) Denver Broncos
11) Detroit Lions
12) Green Bay Packers
13) Houston Texans
14) Indianapolis Colts
15) Jacksonville Jaguars
16) Kansas City Chiefs
17) Miami Dolphins
18) Minnesota Vikings
19) New England Patriots
20) New Orleans Saints
21) New York Giants
22) New York Jets
23) Oakland Raiders
24) Philadelphia Eagles
25) Pittsburgh Steelers
26) San Diego Chargers
27) San Francisco 49ers
28) Seattle Seahawks
29) St. Louis Rams
30) Tampa Bay Buccaneers
31) Tennessee Titans
32) Washington Redskins

Women and Football

There is a strong tradition of women's football in the United States. One of the first times women played organized football was in 1926. The Frankford Yellow Jackets hired women to play at halftime during their NFL games. Since then, there have been many professional and semi-professional women leagues.

In 1965, a businessman named Sid Friedman started a league called the Women's Professional Football League (WPFL). At first, the league had two teams, one in Akron and one in Cleveland. Later, there were teams in Toledo, Buffalo, Pittsburgh, and Toronto, Ontario. Another league called the National Women's Football League (NWFL) was started in 1974. After some early success, interest and attendance dropped.

In 1999, two entertainment promoters, Carter Turner and Terry Sullivan, organized a woman's exhibition game that was played at the Hubert H. Humphrey Metrodome in Minneapolis, Minnesota. Soon, Turner and Sullivan held other games. There was an all-star game at the Orange Bowl in Miami, Florida. This led to the start of the Women's Professional Football League (WPFL). The league has 15 teams in cities such as Houston, New York, Las Vegas, Dallas, and Los Angeles.

The football used in the women's professional leagues is slightly smaller than the ball that is used in the NFL.

The WPFL was invited by the NFL to play an exhibition game during the week of Super Bowl XXXIV. The Dallas Diamonds won three straight WPFL titles from 2004 to 2006. The 2007 WPFL championship game was played in Atlanta, Georgia.

GET CONNECTED

Find more information about women's football at **www.womens profootball.com**.

There are three other professional or semi-professional women's football leagues in the United States. They are the Independent Women's Football League (IWFL), the National Women's Football Association (NWFA), and the Women's Football League (WFL).

All of these leagues hold their own championship games. The Detroit Demolition are the only team to win the NWFA championship three years in a row. The Sacramento Sirens are the only three-time champions of the IWFL.

Some high school girls now play tackle football with the boys on their community or high school teams. Girls play **touch football** and **flag football** in many different leagues. Some leagues have mixed boys' and girls' teams. Other leagues have girls-only teams that play full-contact, tackle football.

Denise Cohen played linebacker for the Minneapolis Vixen of the WPFL.

Katie Hnida
Placekicker

Katie Hnida was the first woman to play National Collegiate Athletic Association (NCAA) Division I Football. She kicked **field goals**, converts, and extra points. Katie played three years of high school football in Littleton, Colorado. She kicked four field goals and 83 extra points in her career at Chatfield High School. In 2003, she made the University of New Mexico (UNM) team as a kicker. Injuries forced her to stop playing, but she returned to play football at UNM in 2007. Hnida has been an inspiration to other girls. She was named the Colorado Sportswoman of the Year. *Teen People Magazine* named her one of America's 20 Most Influential Teens.

Historical Highlights

There have been many historical highlights in the history of the Super Bowl. Some of the best athletes to play the game of football have played in the Super Bowl.

Bart Starr of the Green Bay Packers was the first quarterback to win the Super Bowl. In Super Bowl I, he threw two touchdown passes and was named the first Super Bowl most valuable player (MVP). Starr led the Packers to another Super Bowl victory in Super Bowl II when Green Bay defeated the Oakland Raiders 33–14.

In 1969, New York Jets quarterback Joe Namath led his team to victory in Super Bowl III. The Jets were not expected to win the game. Namath promised the Jets would win the game. They went on to beat Baltimore 16–7 and become the first AFL team to win the Super Bowl.

The Miami Dolphins completed the only perfect season in NFL history when they defeated the Washington Redskins 14–7 in Super Bowl VII. The Dolphins won all of their 14 regular-season games and all three playoff games to finish the year with a 17–0 record.

San Francisco 49ers quarterback Joe Montana often led his team to victory late in the game. In Super Bowl XXIII, the 49ers were trailing the Cincinnati Bengals 16–13. With only 39 seconds left to play, Montana threw a touchdown pass to receiver John Taylor. The 49ers went on to win the game.

Joe Montana is the only player to win the Super Bowl MVP award three times.

In Super Bowl XXXIV, the Tennessee Titans were losing 23–16 to the St. Louis Rams. The Titans drove the ball down to the Rams' 10-yard line. There was only enough time left in the game for one play. Kevin Dyson caught a pass but he was tackled only 1 yard away from the end zone. He stretched as far as he could, but he could not reach the end zone.

John Elway was the quarterback of the Denver Broncos. In Super Bowl XXXII, he made the run of a lifetime. Late in the game, the Broncos needed a first down. Elway took the ball. He ran with the ball and dove head first. Three Green Bay Packers defenders hit him hard. However, Elway made the first down. The Broncos went on to score a touchdown to win the game.

Kevin Dyson of the Tennessee Titans missed scoring the tying touchdown in Super Bowl XXXIV by less than one yard.

SINGLE-GAME SUPER BOWL RECORDS

RECORD	PLAYER	TEAM	YEAR
Passing Attempts – 58	Jim Kelly	Buffalo Bills	1992
Passing Completions – 32	Tom Brady	New England Patriots	2004
Passing Yards – 414	Kurt Warner	St. Louis Rams	2000
Touchdown Passes – 6	Steve Young	San Francisco 49ers	1995
Interceptions – 3	Rod Martin	Oakland Raiders	1981
Catching Yards – 215	Jerry Rice	San Francisco 49ers	1989
Touchdown Catches – 3	Jerry Rice	San Francisco 49ers	1990, 1995
Longest Catch – 85 yards	Muhsin Muhammad	Carolina Panthers	2004
Rushing Attempts – 38	John Riggins	Washington Redskins	1983
Rushing Yards – 204	Tommy Smith	Washington Redskins	1988
Rushing Touchdowns – 3	Terrell Davis	Denver Broncos	1998
Longest Rush – 75 yards	Willie Parker	Pittsburgh Steelers	2006

PASSING RECORDS   RECEIVING RECORDS   RUSHING RECORDS

LEGENDS
and Current Stars

Adam Vinatieri – Placekicker

Adam Vinatieri has been a member of four Super Bowl winning teams. He is known as a clutch kicker. This is because he has made so many game-winning field goals in the final seconds of the game. Vinatieri played for the New England Patriots. His field goals won two Super Bowls. In Super Bowl XXXVI, Vinatieri kicked a 48-yard field goal on the final play to win the game. In Super Bowl XXXVIII, Vinatieri kicked the game-winning field goal with only four seconds left to play. His kick beat the Carolina Panthers 32–29. In 2006, Vinatieri joined the Indianapolis Colts. He helped the Colts defeat the Chicago Bears to win the team's first Super Bowl.

Jerry Rice

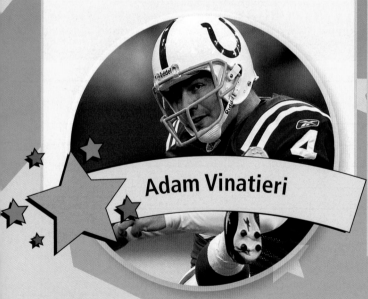

Adam Vinatieri

Jerry Rice – Wide Receiver

Jerry Rice played for San Francisco, Oakland, and Seattle. During his career, Rice set 38 NFL records. They include most touchdowns (208), most receptions (1,549) and most receiving yards (22,895). He holds the NFL record for catching a pass in 274 straight games.

Rice played in four Super Bowls, and his team won three of these. In Super Bowl XXIII, Rice tied the record for most pass catches in a Super Bowl. He caught 11 passes and gained 215 yards. This helped San Francisco defeat Cincinnati. Other Super Bowl records Rice set during his career include most total yards gained (589) and the most total number of touchdowns scored (8).

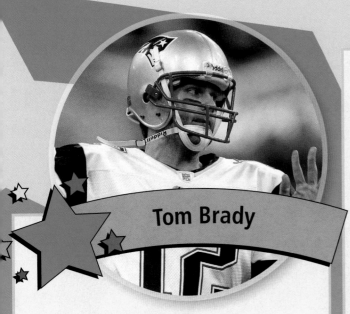

Tom Brady

Lawrence Taylor – Linebacker

Lawrence Taylor was a linebacker for the New York Giants. He changed the way the position was played. Before he joined the league, linebackers were usually big and slow. Taylor was fast enough to cover receivers and strong enough to block any offensive lineman.

Taylor had good balance and quick feet. This helped him avoid blockers and tackle the opposing team's quarterback. This type of play is called a quarterback sack. Taylor had more than 132 sacks in his 13 seasons in the NFL.

In 1986, he became only the second linebacker to win the NFL's most valuable player award. He was named as the NFL's Defensive Player of the Year a record three times. Taylor helped the Giants win three Super Bowl titles.

Tom Brady – Quarterback

Tom Brady is the quarterback of the New England Patriots. He has led his team to victory in three Super Bowls. Twice, Brady has been named the Super Bowl's most valuable player.

Brady was the first quarterback to win three NFL championships before the age of 28. He has one of the best win-loss records in NFL playoff history. Brady has won 12 playoff games and lost only two during his career. He is known for coming up with big plays. Brady completes important passes when the game is on the line. He holds the NFL record for most pass completions in a Super Bowl game. In Super Bowl XXXVIII, Brady completed a record 32 passes. This performance helped New England defeat Carolina 32–29.

Lawrence Taylor

Famous Firts

Herb Adderley of the Green Bay Packers was the first player to score a touchdown after intercepting a pass. He ran the ball 60 yards down the field to help the Packers beat the Oakland Raiders in Super Bowl II.

The first tickets with the words "Super Bowl" printed on them were sold for Super Bowl IV in 1970. The tickets cost $15.

In Super Bowl XVII, Miami's Fulton Walker became the first player to return a kickoff for a touchdown. He caught the opening kickoff of the second quarter and took it all the way down the field to help the Dolphins defeat the Washington Redskins 27–17.

Doug Williams was the first African American quarterback to win the Super Bowl MVP award. He helped lead the Washington Redskins to a 42–10 victory over Denver in Super Bowl XXII.

San Francisco's Roger Craig was the first player to score three touchdowns in a Super Bowl game. He did it in Super Bowl XIX.

Dallas' Chuck Howley was the first defensive player and the first player from a losing team to be named Super Bowl MVP. This happened in Super Bowl V.

Charles Haley was the first player to win five Super Bowl titles. He won two titles with San Francisco and three with Dallas.

Doug Williams became the head football coach at Grambling University after retiring as a player.

Roger Craig won three Super Bowl titles as a member of the San Francisco 49ers.

Washington's Timmy Smith became the first player to rush for more than 200 yards in Super Bowl XXII. Smith scored two touchdowns in the Redskins 42–10 win over the Denver Broncos in Super Bowl XXII.

Terry Bradshaw was the first quarterback to throw four touchdowns in the Super Bowl. He helped Pittsburgh beat Dallas 35–31 in Super Bowl XIII.

The Baltimore Colts' Tom Matte was the first player to rush for 100 yards in a Super Bowl game. He did it against the New York Jets in Super Bowl III.

The Oakland Raiders were the first wild card team to win the Super Bowl. They scored a 27–10 victory over Philadelphia in Super Bowl XV.

Oakland's Rod Martin was the first player to have three interceptions in one championship game. His three interceptions during Super Bowl XV helped the Raiders defeat the Philadelphia Eagles 27–10.

Tom Matte averaged a Super Bowl-record 10.5 yards per run for the Baltimore Colts in Super Bowl III. He was a quarterback at Ohio State University before becoming a running back in the NFL.

The First Championship Game

The first NFL championship game was played in 1932. Before that, the team with the best winning percentage was named champion. In 1932, Chicago and Portsmouth were tied. An extra game was needed to decide the champion. On the day of the game, it was cold and snowy in Chicago. The league felt more fans would attend the game if it was held indoors. They decided to play the game at Chicago Stadium. It was best known as a hockey and boxing arena. Truckloads of dirt were brought in to cover the concrete floor. The field was only 80 yards (73 m) long. Both teams used one set of goal posts. They were on the goal line. More than 10,000 fans watched the Bears win the game 9–0.

The Rise of the Super Bowl

1920

The first professional football league, the American Professional Football Association (APFA), is created. This league would change its name to the National Football League (NFL) on June 24, 1922.

1921

Official league statistics are compiled. The team with the best winning percentage is named champion.

1932

The first NFL championship game is played. The Chicago Bears beat the Portsmouth Spartans 9–0.

1950

The Los Angeles Rams become the first team to have all of their games shown on television.

1951

The NFL Championship Game is televised for the first time across the United States.

1958

Baltimore beats the New York Giants 23–17 in the only championship game in NFL history to go into overtime.

1959

A new professional football league called the American Football League (AFL) is formed.

1960

Pete Rozelle is named commissioner of the NFL. Lamar Hunt (below) becomes president of the AFL.

1967

Super Bowl I takes place on January 15, 1967. The Green Bay Packers defeat the Kansas City Chiefs 35–10.

1969

An AFL team wins the Super Bowl for the first time. The New York Jets defeat the Baltimore Colts 16–7.

1970

The AFL and NFL merge. The league has two conferences, the AFC and the NFC.

2006

The Pittsburgh Steelers become the first team to win five Super Bowl titles.

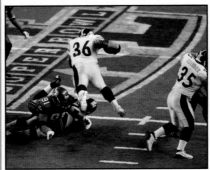

2007

Tony Dungy of the Indianapolis Colts becomes the first African American head coach to win the Super Bowl.

QUICK FACTS

- Super Bowl XXXVIII, on February 1, 2004, was the most watched television program ever. More than 144,400,000 people from around the world watched the game.

- Mike Ditka, Tom Flores, and Tony Dungy have won the Super Bowl as players and as coaches.

- Bob Hayes is the only person to win an Olympic gold medal and a Super Bowl championship. He won a gold medal in the 100–meter dash at the 1964 Olympics and won the Super Bowl with the Dallas Cowboys in 1971.

Test Your Knowledge

1 What team won Super Bowl I?

2 Which team has the made the most Super Bowl appearances?

3 What was the first AFL team to win the Super Bowl?

4 Who is the Super Bowl trophy named after?

5 What two cities have hosted the most Super Bowl games?

6 Who is the only player from the losing team to be named Super Bowl MVP?

7 Who was the first woman to play a game of NCAA Division I football?

8 Who has scored the most Super Bowl touchdowns?

9 Who has been a member of the most Super Bowl-winning teams?

10 What team was the first to have all their games shown on television?

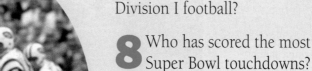

ANSWERS: 1) the Green Bay Packers 2) the Dallas Cowboys 3) the New York Jets 4) Vince Lombardi 5) Miami and New Orleans 6) Chuck Howley 7) Katie Hnida 8) Jerry Rice 9) Charles Haley 10) the Los Angeles Rams

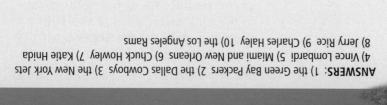

Further Research

Many books and websites provide information on the Super Bowl. To learn more about the tournament, borrow books from the library, or surf the Internet.

Books to Read

Most libraries have computers that connect to a database for researching information. If you input a key word, you will be provided with a list of books in the library that contain information on that topic. Non-fiction books are arranged numerically, using their call number. Fiction books are organized alphabetically by the author's last name.

Online Sites

The official NFL web site, **www.nfl.com**, contains information about the history, rules, legends, and stars of the game of football.

You can find video clips, interviews, commentary, and anecdotes about the Super Bowl at **http://ag.nfl.com**.

The official site of Super Bowl, **www.superbowl.com**, has stories, statistics, highlights, and pictures about the history of the Super Bowl.

Glossary

bye: going to the next round of a playoff series without playing an opponent

cleats: spikes on the bottom of football shoes that give a player better traction on muddy and wet fields

end zone: the 10-yard area at both ends of the football field

field goals: kicking the football through the goal posts to score points

flag football: game where a player's progress is stopped when the flag or marker they are wearing is grabbed by the opposing team

fumble: to lose control of the ball

interception: a thrown or passed ball that is caught by a member of the opposite team

line of scrimmage: the imaginary line that marks how far the offense has advanced

offside: crossing the line of scrimmage before the ball is snapped

plays: plans of action to move the ball down the field

snap: the movement of the football from the ground to the quarterback's hands on the line of scrimmage

synthetic: not made from natural materials

touch football: game where a player is touched instead of tackled

Index